THE WINE AND WISDOM SERIES No.1

# A TWO BERTH LIFE

## A One Act Play

## Lynn Brittney

Published by Playstage
United Kingdom.

An imprint of Write Publications Ltd

**www.playsforadults.com**

Designed by Kate Lowe, Greensands Graphics
Printed by Creeds Ltd, Bridport, Dorset

# Note to producers about staging "A Two-Berth Life"

The action takes place in the interior of an old-fashioned small caravan. In order to suggest this lack of space (and the fact that the actors climb up and down from the caravan), it therefore lends itself to being constructed on a moveable or fixed rostrum (depending upon whether this play is performed as part of a one act festival or is combined with another one act play to make an in-house production).

One suggestion would be to make the back of the set with a curved top so that it suggests the shape of a caravan. The rest can be done with the typical built-in look of the furniture of the inside of a caravan, making liberal use of wood-effect Formica finishes and garish fabric colours for the cushions and curtains. A built-in toilet compartment is required but the door can be on the side, so that the audience cannot see the interior and it, therefore, can be completely empty. There also needs to be a tiny worktop on which an electric kettle can be seen to be used. It would be a nice touch to actually have an electricity supply to the set, so that a small portable TV can be on and a kettle can be boiled, but it is not essential. The TV can be angled away from the audience and the kettle does not have to actually boil.

As the text explains, there are various props needed, that you will have to find space for – like a chair; a folded up wheelchair; a medical drip on a stand; and a wooden ramp to fit over the stairs in and out of the "caravan".

While the idea of setting a play in a caravan may seem initially daunting, it is, in fact, really quite simple.

# WINE AND WISDOM 1 : A TWO BERTH LIFE

## CAST *(In order of appearance)*

| | |
|---|---|
| DEN | Northerner, age range 50 – 65, terminally ill |
| GLORIA | Den's wife, also a northerner, same age range |
| PAULA | Their daughter, a nurse, very practical, age range 30-40 |
| BRIAN | Their son, a bit dozy, a few years younger than Paula |

2 male and 2 female parts.

*The action takes place in Den and Gloria's caravan. The text tells us that they are parked in the car park of a village hall somewhere in Derbyshire and are attending a Caravan Club holiday/get-together. It is the Club's Quiz Night.*

# WINE AND WISDOM 1
## A TWO-BERTH LIFE

*The setting is the interior of a small caravan. There is a fitted bed in the wall of the caravan, facing the audience. DEN is asleep on this bed, fully dressed, propped up on several pillows and covered by a travel rug. He is attached to a portable drip on a stand. There is a small television, flickering but silent on a formica top at the foot of the bed. Behind DEN'S head are some fitted cupboards with a small sink and tap set in and a hob next to it. There is a wheelchair in front of it. Then there is a toilet compartment. Beyond that is a small seating area with a fitted table for dining. On it is a newspaper, some reading glasses and a pen. The entrance door is at the foot of DEN'S bed. Outside the entrance door is also part of the set. (See suggested set plan) GLORIA enters quietly, sees that DEN is asleep and gingerly goes into the toilet. There is a pause, then we hear the toilet flushing. DEN opens his eyes and GLORIA comes out of the toilet.*

| | |
|---|---|
| GLORIA | Oh damn! I've gone and woken you, love. I am sorry. |
| DEN | No, you're alright. I was just dozing. |
| GLORIA | I had to come in and use the lav. There was such a queue in the hall. Anyway, I was going to come in and see you anyway. It's half time. Paula's going to bring us our ploughman's in here. |
| DEN | Oh I don't know that I'm that hungry. |
| GLORIA | Oh you can manage a bit of cheese, I'm sure you can, love. It's Wensleydale. Your favourite. |
| DEN | *(struggling to sit up a bit. GLORIA helps him)* How's the quiz going? |

GLORIA     Champion. Our Brian's dead quick with them answers and
           our Paula got all the questions in the Pop Music round.
           They don't need me really. I know nowt about pop music,
           or films, or geography.

DEN        Eeh lass…you ought to know a bit about geography, at
           least. Considering the places we've been in this caravan!

GLORIA     Ah, well I would if it was British geography but it's all
           foreign stuff.

DEN        Oh.

GLORIA     Anyway, I've got summat here that you can help us with.

DEN        Oh aye? What's that then?

GLORIA     We've all been given this sheet of questions to do in the
           supper-break. Very hard they are. I said to Paula "Give em
           here and let's get your Dad to do them. He'll know what's
           what."

DEN        Let's have a look at them then.

           (GLORIA gets a sheet out of her handbag and gives it to him)

GLORIA     You have a look at those while I put a brew on.

DEN        Oh yes. I'm as dry as the bottom of a budgie's cage.

GLORIA     Aaw. I should have popped back sooner.

DEN        No, you're alright. I was asleep anyway.

GLORIA     (filling up a kettle at the tap and putting it on the hob)
           How was the football?

DEN        Bloody awful. They just ponced about on that field for the
           first half. I'm bloody glad I'm not a season ticket holder
           anymore. I'd be asking for my money back, that's for sure. I
           haven't seen one decent game from them so far.

| | |
|---|---|
| GLORIA | What happened in the second half? |
| DEN | Dunno. I fell asleep, it was that boring. Might as well turn the telly off now, love. |
| GLORIA | *(turning off the television)* Have you looked at those questions? |
| DEN | Get my specs love. I can't see owt nowadays. |
| GLORIA | *(she retrieves his spectacles from the dining table)* Comes to us all, love. Nothing special about your eyes. I can't read the paper anymore without glasses on. |
| DEN | *(putting his glasses on and reading the sheet)* So what have we here? |
| GLORIA | I can't make head nor tail of it. |
| DEN | Question 1. Three C's in a F. |
| GLORIA | See? It's all like that. Just numbers and initials. I said to Paula "The only one who can decipher this is your Dad. He's the Cryptic Crossword King. He'll know what it's all about." |
| DEN | Oh yes. It's dead simple. Look. Three C's in a F – Three Coins in a Fountain! |
| GLORIA | Yeah? |
| DEN | Yeah. Question two. A S in T, S 9. A Stitch in Time saves Nine! |
| GLORIA | Oh I get it now! You clever old thing! Your brain never ceases to amaze me! |
| DEN | Oh yes. The brain is working alright, it's just the rest that is crap. |
| GLORIA | Here. Have your tea, Mastermind, and stop feeling sorry for yourself. |

| | |
|---|---|
| DEN | Thanks Glo. Give us a pen, would you? I'd best write these answers down. |
| | *(GLORIA gets a pen from the dining table and then sits down in the wheelchair)* |
| DEN | Right. Question three. *(He takes sip from his tea)* Bye, that tea's lovely. Must be the water in Derbyshire. |
| GLORIA | Yes. It's very soft. I'm glad the Caravan Club came here again. It's a lovely location. Beautiful scenery and the hall is really good. Nice toilets, smashing kitchen. Better than that place we all went to last year in Wales. |
| DEN | Oh, I don't know. I like Wales. It was just that it was a bad time for us, that's all. Me being diagnosed just before we went. |
| GLORIA | Yes. What's Question three then? |
| DEN | 5 GR. |
| GLORIA | Go on then. Amaze me again. What's the answer? |
| DEN | Five gold rings! You know, from the Twelve Days of Christmas. Hold up! I bet that's one of the other questions *(He scans the sheet.)* ...yep! There it is! Question 14. 12 D of C. Hey, hey! Cracked two at once! I haven't lost it, Glo. |
| GLORIA | No, love. You haven't lost it. Do you want to come in to the hall for the second half? Now you've had a bit of a sleep, we can put you in the wheelchair and take you over. |
| DEN | No. |
| GLORIA | It would be alright, love. We can always pop you back if you get tired. |

| | |
|---|---|
| DEN | No. Anyway, there's a programme I want to watch at half-past. |
| GLORIA | It's not another one of those medical documentaries is it? They only upset you. |
| DEN | No! It's about the great Bobby Charlton. It's all about his career. I can't miss that. |
| GLORIA | You and your football. Have a go at another question. We could win this with you doing them all. |
| DEN | What's the prize? |
| GLORIA | Twenty pounds. |
| DEN | Oh, not to be sneezed at then. Right, let's have another look. Question 4. 12 G M and T. Now that's a tricky one. 12 G M and T.... 12 G M and T. No, I'll go back to that one. Question 5. 3 B M. Oh yes! Easy peasy. |
| GLORIA | Go on then, genius, amaze me. |
| DEN | Three Blind Mice! |
| | *(GLORIA laughs. PAULA enters with two cheese ploughman's on plates)* |
| PAULA | Here you are, Mum. Two ploughman's with extra pickle for Dad. |
| GLORIA | Give us em here love. *(GLORIA takes the ploughmans and puts one on the fitted cupboards and keeps one on her lap.)* |
| PAULA | How yah feeling Dad? |
| DEN | *(resigned)* Same as always love, so there's no point in asking. |
| PAULA | Let's have a look at that drip of yours. Make sure it's working OK. |

| | |
|---|---|
| GLORIA | Let me move out of the way first. |
| PAULA | God there's no room in here, is there? I always forget how small this caravan is. *(She fiddles with the drip, checking all the connections and the bandage on DEN'S hand)* |
| DEN | It was plenty big enough for all of us when you were little. |
| GLORIA | Well, it wasn't really, Den. We just didn't mind, that's all. It was a squash but, bye, we had some good times in this old thing. |
| PAULA | Yeah, we had some terrible times too! Do you remember the year when we went to the Lakes and we were parked in that site on the hill? |
| GLORIA | Ooh yes! And it tipped it down all week. Then one night, your Dad got up to go to the lav – cos he'd had his usual skinful in the pub – and the whole bloody caravan slid down the hill in a mudslide! |
| | *(They all start laughing)* |
| DEN | And there's me, on the bog, with me trousers round me ankles, and the caravan's rolling down the hill and I'm thinking "I've got to give up the beer – it's just too bloody strong." I thought it was me! I thought I was so blind drunk that everything was moving! |
| PAULA | Mind you. I never felt a thing. |
| GLORIA | No, you never woke up. I couldn't believe that. When the caravan stopped moving you were practically standing on your head, but you never woke up. |
| PAULA | Well it was such a tight squeeze. You and me in the bed and Dad and Brian on the floor – the caravan could have done a loop the loop and I wouldn't have felt owt! |

| | |
|---|---|
| DEN | Aye, I know. We should have bought a bigger caravan when you two came along. A two-berther was just too small. |
| GLORIA | No. Best contraceptive I ever had! |
| PAULA | Mum! |
| GLORIA | Well it was! Every weekend and most of the summer holidays, it was you and me in the bed and Brian and your dad on the floor. Never needed to take the pill! |
| PAULA | I'm embarrassed now. |
| | *(DEN and GLORIA laugh)* |
| DEN | Embarrassed!?! And you a nurse and all. You shouldn't be embarrassed by owt! |
| PAULA | It's different when it's your own parents. |
| GLORIA | 'Ere, your Dad's getting on a treat with them questions. |
| PAULA | Are you, Dad? |
| DEN | Dead easy. How long have I got with them? |
| PAULA | The Chairman says that they don't have to be handed in until the end of the quiz. So plenty of time. |
| DEN | Champion. |
| GLORIA | Hadn't you better get back to that husband of yours, Paula? The appetite he's got, he'll eat your ploughman's as well, if you leave him alone for too long. |
| PAULA | That's true. He's already been back to our caravan twice, Dad, to get some more peanuts and crisps. |
| DEN | Ah, he's a big strapping lad, your Peter. Needs his nourishment for all that rugby he plays. |
| PAULA | Right, well I'll go back then. Do you fancy a beer Dad? Do |

|  | you good? How about if Brian pops over a bit later with a Guinness? |
|---|---|
| DEN | Aye, alright then. Just a half though. Can't manage more than a half. |
| PAULA | Right. See you in a bit. *(PAULA leaves and GLORIA goes and sits back next to DEN)* |
| GLORIA | She's a good girl. |
| DEN | Yes. I'm glad you'll have her to look after you when I'm gone. |
| GLORIA | Now, that's enough! I don't like that talk and you know it! We don't speak about you being gone, because you're not going anywhere yet. Anyway, who says I need looking after? I've never needed looking after! |
| DEN | I was thinking, just now, when our Paula was talking, that I've not done right by you really, have I Gloria? |
| GLORIA | What ever do you mean? |
| DEN | Well, the caravan, like. It seems to sum up our life, doesn't it? Just a two-berth life. We couldn't afford owt else and we never seemed to just get up to a four-berth-life. |
| GLORIA | Don't talk soft. Did I ever complain? Did I? |
| DEN | Well, no. |
| GLORIA | Well then shut up. One of the worst things about your illness is that you get so maudlin. You just listen here. We've had some wonderful times in this caravan. We've traveled all over the place, we've made friends, good friends in the Caravan Club. Friends that are waiting in that hall now, to see you. Asking after you. We've had great times as a family in this caravan. We've laughed and laughed'til I |

thought I would wet my knickers and, until you got ill, I can never remember – never – a time in our marriage when you made me cry. That's worth all them fancy houses, foreign holidays and big caravans put together. A two-berth life indeed! I've had a four star luxury life with you, from my point of view. We've had food on the table, clothes on us backs and plenty of love. If you do die, Den, and I stress *if*, you can rest in peace, knowing that God will judge you as a wonderful father and husband. *(She gets her hanky out and wipes away a few tears and blows her nose)*

*(There is a small silence)*

DEN        Twelve Good Men and True.

GLORIA     Eh?

DEN        The answer to question number four. Twelve Good Men and True. That's what they used to call a jury. It was what you said about God's judgement that brought it to me.

GLORIA     You daft pillock. I'm sitting here pouring my heart out and you're not listening to a blind word I've said. Your mind's just on them questions. Men!

DEN        Oy, oy! You just said I was a wonderful husband!

GLORIA     *(laughing)* Oh, give us a cuddle.

           *(They hug)*

GLORIA     Now, sit up a bit more and eat your ploughman's. I won't take no for an answer. *(She helps him sit up a bit more. Then she gives him the plate and he begins to pick at it.)*

DEN        Right. Well you can go back to the quiz, if you want, and leave me to solve these questions.

GLORIA     No. You're alright. The kids can manage without me. I'd sooner sit here with you.

DEN        Please yourself but you'll have to work for the privilege.

GLORIA     Cheeky monkey. What do you mean?

DEN        Well I can't eat and read at the same time. You read out the questions to me and I'll answer them.

GLORIA     Wait while I get my glasses. *(She fiddles around in her handbag and puts on her specs)* Right let's have a look. Question five. Eight L's on a S.

DEN        Um...eight legs on a spider?

GLORIA     The man is undefeated. Next. Seven S. Yes, that's right, just S. Seven S.

DEN        Hang on while I taste a bit of this Wensleydale. Hey, it's not bad! Must be nice and strong if I can taste it.

GLORIA     Yes. I tried a bit while we were making the ploughman's this afternoon. I said to Paula "This cheese is nice and strong. Your Dad'll be able to taste it." And I was right.

DEN        Seven samurai. Seven S is seven samurai.

GLORIA     I'd better write these down. Give us the pen. *(She writes)* Eight legs on a spider. Seven Samurai. How d'you spell samurai?

DEN        S..a..m..u..r..a..i. You'd better write down twelve good men and true as well. Number four wasn't it?

GLORIA     Yep. Question number seven. 12 A.

DEN        Twelve apostles.

GLORIA     OK. Wait while I eat something. Ooh, this bread's lovely and fresh. I like nice, soft bread. Have a bit.

| | |
|---|---|
| DEN | I will. I could do with another cup of tea though. |
| GLORIA | Righto. Have another question to mull over while I put the kettle on. Question eight. Fifteen M on a D M's C. |
| DEN | Ems? |
| GLORIA | Yes. Have a look. M apostrophe S. Ems. |
| DEN | Ems. |
| GLORIA | The Caravan Club's going to go to Scarborough next month. Shall I sign us up? |
| DEN | Ems. What? |
| GLORIA | I said, the Caravan Club is going to go to Scarborough next month. Shall I sign us up? Nice bit of sea air would do you good. Nice flat promenade there too, for pushing the wheelchair along. What d'you think? |
| DEN | I don't know. I might not be here next month. |
| GLORIA | Why where are you going? |
| DEN | You know what I mean. |
| GLORIA | I do and I'm not paying it any mind. Shall we go to Scarborough or not? I say yes, because we haven't been there since the year Paula was born. I quite fancy having a look at it again. |
| DEN | Well, if you fancy it, I suppose we'll do it. Go on then. If I'm here or not it doesn't matter. |
| GLORIA | Oh, little Nelly on her death bed! Give it a rest. Have you solved that question yet? |
| DEN | Death bed....you said death bed.... |
| GLORIA | I was only joking... |

| DEN | No, that helped me solve it. Fifteen Men on a Dead Man's Chest. |
|---|---|
| GLORIA | Oh my God! I'm glad I'm of some use. |
| DEN | Yes, Glo, you just keep wittering away woman and we'll soon have these questions sorted. |
| GLORIA | Here's your tea. Right, now, I'll have another mouthful of cheese and press on with question nine. *(Pause while she munches and DEN sips his tea)* Question nine. Seventy Six T. Oh even I know that one. |
| BOTH OF THEM | Seventy six trombones! |
| GLORIA | We're doing well here. |
| | *(BRIAN appears with a half pint of Guinness)* |
| DEN | Hello son. Is that my Guinness? |
| BRIAN | Yeah.  I just popped out before they start up again. Paula says do you know the answer to one of the film questions. She couldn't get it. |
| DEN | Go on then. What is it? |
| BRIAN | Name the seven actors who played The Magnificent Seven. |
| DEN and GLORIA | Brad Dexter! |
| BRIAN | Eh? |
| DEN | That's the one that everyone always forgets. They always remember Yul Brynner, Steve McQueen, Horst Bucholz, James Coburn, Robert Vaughn and Clint Walker. But they never remember Brad Dexter. Poor bugger. Fancy going through life being the one that everyone always forgets. |

| | |
|---|---|
| BRIAN | Right. |
| GLORIA | Is Hannah enjoying herself? |
| BRIAN | Yeah. Seems to be. |
| GLORIA | Nicest girlfriend you've ever had, Brian. You don't want to let that one slip through your fingers. |
| BRIAN | Yeah. Well...actually...I was thinking about.... |
| GLORIA | *(beaming)* Are you really?! |
| DEN | Glo, let the poor lad get a word out, will ya? Go on son. |
| BRIAN | Well I was thinking about asking her to marry me. What do you think? |
| GLORIA | Eeh, give us a hug! *(She hugs him and DEN smiles)* |
| BRIAN | Don't be daft mum. She might not say yes. |
| GLORIA | Of course she will. She'll bite your hand off. Nice looking lad like you with a great career. She's a nice girl. I've got a good feeling about this one. |
| BRIAN | What do you mean "this one"? I haven't had that many. |
| DEN | No. That's true. But amongst the favoured few have been some right weirdos. |
| BRIAN | Yeah, I suppose. |
| GLORIA | Ooh yes. I still haven't recovered from Marianne the Goth. She used to terrify the life out of me when she used to just appear in the kitchen with them black eyes and black lips. Must have been like going to bed with the Vampire Queen! |
| BRIAN | Mum! |
| DEN | Hey up, Glo, you're embarrassing our other child now! |
| GLORIA | *(taking a large chunk of BRIAN'S cheek in between her* |

*fingers and wobbling it.)* Is your old mum embarrassing you, eh? Aaw, never mind. Before you know it, you'll be doing the same to your kids.

DEN    Put him down, Glo, and let him get back to the others. Only…son…don't pop the question in the middle of the quiz. It's not very romantic.

GLORIA    Huh! And this from a man who asked me to marry him when I was buying a pound of broken biscuits in Huddersfield market!

BRIAN    You never!

DEN    I know, I know. But I was very shy and I figured I'd ask your mother to do the deed in a place where I wouldn't be expected to go down on one knee.

GLORIA    Oh that was the reason was it?

DEN    It was.

BRIAN    Dad. Paula says that you should come to the second half of the quiz. She says she can take the drip out for an hour or so.

DEN    Oh does she.

GLORIA    I've already mentioned it to your father but he won't budge. *(To DEN)* Everyone's asking after you, you know. Charlie Ackroyd was right put out when I said you weren't coming in.

DEN    I don't want people feeling sorry for me.

GLORIA    Sorry for you! You daft pillock! Who's going to feel sorry for you? You've known these people for too long, Den. They won't feel sorry for you. Especially when you get all the questions right and win the hamper.

| | |
|---|---|
| DEN | Oh it's a hamper is it? |
| BRIAN | Yeah. It's a really good one as well. You've got to come, Dad. Round 8 is questions on the 1950's and none of us can answer them. |
| DEN | 1950's? I'll think about it. |
| | *(GLORIA breaks into a big smile but decides to take a "softly, softly" approach)* |
| GLORIA | Well you get back there, our Brian, and tell Paula to pop back in a bit to take that drip out. |
| DEN | I haven't said anything definite yet. |
| GLORIA | No, I know. But it won't do any harm for that drip to come out for a while. Paula said she needed to put it on the other hand today anyway. |
| BRIAN | Right, well I'll be off. See ya in a bit. |
| | *(He leaves and GLORIA hugs DEN)* |
| GLORIA | Ooh, another wedding in the family! What about that then? |
| DEN | Very good. Very good indeed. This Hannah's the first one he's ever brought on one of our caravan holidays, isn't she? |
| GLORIA | Yes. Well all the others were too stuck-up. They wanted fancy hotels, not caravans. |
| DEN | Good job our Paula's got the room in her caravan. |
| GLORIA | Oh yes. Well it's good for the youngsters to be together anyway. More fun. Eat some more of your ploughman's. |
| DEN | No. I've had enough, thanks. |
| GLORIA | Well drink a bit of the Guinness. |
| DEN | Aye, alright. *(He takes a sip)* Nice drop of Guinness, this. |

We'd better crack on with a few more of them questions.

GLORIA    Righto. Question ten.  10 F and 10 T.

DEN    Ten fingers and ten toes.

GLORIA    By God, you're sharp tonight. Question eleven. 4 A of the A.

DEN    Dunno. I'll think about that one.

GLORIA    Question twelve. 2 FT.

DEN    You should know this one, Glo.

GLORIA    Should I ? Why?

DEN    Bingo.

GLORIA    Oh! Two Fat Ladies!

DEN    There you go.

GLORIA    I wish I had a brain like yours.

DEN    You do. You just don't concentrate, that's all.

GLORIA    No. My mum used to say I was a "flibberty-gibbet" – whatever that means.

DEN    Don't quote your mother at me, for God's sake.

GLORIA    She wasn't that bad.

DEN    Huh! She was like something out of a Dicken's novel. Never had her head out of the Bible. Always going to those spiritualists meetings. How you ever grew up to be so normal I don't know. Ah!

GLORIA    What is it love? Are you in pain?

DEN    No. Talking about your mother and her Bible. Four Acts of the Apostles. The answer to question eleven.

GLORIA    Now see, that's what I mean. Your brain works in a totally different way to other people's. I reckon, if you'd had the education, you would have been recognized as a genius and you'd have been something wonderful – like a professor or summat.

DEN Don't be daft.

GLORIA You would. God's honest truth. You amaze everyone. They all say so.

DEN Who says that?

GLORIA Well Charlie Ackroyd for a start. He's always going on about how clever you are.

DEN Well, compared to him, God bless him, I am a ruddy genius.

*(GLORIA giggles)*

GLORIA Don't be unkind.

DEN No. Well. He's a lovely soul but you and I know that he's a few pence short of a shilling.

GLORIA He got lost on his way here again.

DEN Well, that proves my point. I mean this is only the third time the Caravan Club has come here and he still can't find his way. I'm enjoying this Guinness.

GLORIA Good for you. Now, Question thirteen. I P in a PT.

DEN Now I should have spotted that one earlier when I got the five gold rings. It's a partridge in a pear tree. I bet there's another one of those in there somewhere. Have a look, Glo. Is there 2 TD?

GLORIA No.

| | |
|---|---|
| DEN | How about 3 FH? |
| GLORIA | Wait a minute. Yes! Question twenty. |
| DEN | There you are. Three French hens. So we've done that one and I did question fourteen earlier, didn't I? |
| GLORIA | Yes. |
| DEN | So there's only six more to do. |
| GLORIA | Let's crack on then, so we get them done before you go in the hall. |
| DEN | I haven't said yes, yet. |
| GLORIA | Don't be stubborn Den. You as good as said you would to our Brian. |
| | Now question fifteen. 4 H of the A. |
| DEN | Four Horsemen of the Apocalypse. |
| GLORIA | What the hell is that? |
| DEN | You know. War, Famine, something and Death. I think it's Plague and Death. Not sure. |
| GLORIA | Oh very cheerful! Is there anything you don't know, Den? |
| | *(There is a pause)* |
| DEN | Yes. I don't know when I'm going to die. |
| GLORIA | It'll be right this minute, if you don't shut up. What sort of a thing is that to say? |
| DEN | No, but seriously. I wonder if you do know when it's going to happen. Like animals do. You know. You just wake up one morning and you know that it's your last day. |
| GLORIA | *(struggling to hold back her tears)* My dad always used to say that you should live each day as though it were your |

last. That you should never go to bed on a cross word and that you should try and fill each day with as much joy as you can. And you've done that Den. God knows you've done that. You've always been cheerful. Always been positive. Even when I was ill after the birth of our Brian, you never let me get really bad. And I'm going to do the same for you. You're going to keep going, love. D'you hear me? Last year, the doctors gave you six months and, look! Here you are, large as life and twice as ugly. Now, question sixteen, and lets hope this is not another bloody morbid answer.

DEN         You're a tough woman Gloria.

GLORIA      Ooh God! Now I know I'm in trouble when you call me Gloria. That's your "you've overspent the housekeeping again" name for me. You always call me Glo.

DEN         It always seemed the right name for you – "Glo" – 'cos when I first saw you, that's what you did – you glowed.

GLORIA      I was probably hot and sweaty after my shift in the factory.

DEN         *(laughing)* By God, you were that! Eight hours of boiling jam and you used to slip out of my embrace like a wet mackerel!

GLORIA      *(laughing too)* Oh and I suppose you were better than me, in your greasy overalls, all covered in brake fluid!?!

DEN         What a pair! A grease monkey and a jam boiler!

GLORIA      Oy, less of the boiler, if you please!

DEN         No, but seriously, you did glow – from inside, like. Like a beam of sunshine. You still do.

GLORIA          But I don't smell of strawberry jam anymore, eh?

DEN             No, but I still can't open a jar of the stuff without wanting
                a bit of the other!

                *(GLORIA shrieks)*

GLORIA          You should be locked up!

                *(PAULA appears)*

PAULA           Well, I'm glad someone's having a good time! We're getting
                caned in there!

GLORIA          Are you love? What's amiss then?

PAULA           Bloody Brian, that's what. He only proposed to Hannah
                and ruined the last round.

DEN             He never! I told him not to do it at the quiz!

GLORIA          Oh bless him! He probably couldn't wait! Impatient, like
                his Dad. How did he do it then?

PAULA           He wrote her a note.

GLORIA and
DEN             No!

PAULA           He did. He scribbles this note and passes it over the table to
                her. Next thing I know, she's crying. So I glare at him and
                say "What have you done now, Brian!" He's all pink in the
                face, staring at her, like he's going to bust. Then she wipes
                her tears away, grabs his hand and says "Yes." He knocks
                over the table and takes her into this big clinch and we
                missed the last four questions, it was such a to do.

GLORIA          Oh my God – she said yes!

PAULA           She must be barmy. I wouldn't have him if he was wrapped in pink ribbon with a million dollar note stuck in his gob.

DEN      Nay, he's a good lad.

PAULA      He's gormless, Dad. What sort of a half-wit proposes by note in the middle of a quiz night?

GLORIA      Er...excuse me...but wasn't it your husband who proposed during half – time at a rugby match.

DEN      Aye. He runs to the line, spits his gumshield out into his hand and says "How about it Paula? Do you fancy getting hitched?" George Clooney's got nothing in your Peter, has he?

PAULA      Yeah, alright. I suppose I can't talk. Anyway, am I to take this drip out, or what? You'll have to come in the hall now Dad. We're three points behind Harry Miller's team and we've got the fifties round coming up next.

DEN      Three points behind Harry Miller? By God! I can't leave this family alone for five minutes, can I? Glo – get me shoes and socks. Paula, get this bloody drip out.

GLORIA      Yes, sir!

*(GLORIA goes and gets his shoes and socks and PAULA starts taking the bandage off his hand and takes the drip out. Then she helps DEN to sit up straight, while GLORIA puts his shoes and socks on. It is obvious that every movement causes DEN a lot of pain. But he is determined.)*

DEN      Gloria....

GLORIA      Oh stop with the Gloria business – it makes me nervous.

DEN      Sorry – Glo...

GLORIA      Yes love.

| | |
|---|---|
| DEN | Rattle off them last four questions to me. I want to get them out of the way before I go in that hall. |
| GLORIA | Right. |
| PAULA | Hurry up Dad. They're just having a ten minute break. |
| DEN | It won't take me a minute. |
| GLORIA | Question sixteen. 21 S in a G. |
| DEN | Twenty one shillings in a guinea. |
| GLORIA | Question seventeen. 1 for S and 2 for J. |
| DEN | One for sorrow and two for joy. |
| PAULA | What the hell is that, when it's at home? |
| DEN | The rhyme about magpies. One for sorrow two for joy... and so on. |
| PAULA | Take your word for it. |
| GLORIA | Question eighteen. 24 B in a P. |
| DEN | 24 blackbirds in a pie. |
| GLORIA | And the last question. 13 in a BD. |
| DEN | Thirteen in a baker's dozen. |
| GLORIA | *(Punching the air)* Yes! Give the man a medal! |
| DEN | I've still got it, haven't I love? |
| GLORIA | In spades, you old bugger. In spades. |
| PAULA | Right. Let's get you to the door. Mum, fold up the wheelchair and get it outside. |

*(PAULA helps DEN, inch by inch to the door. Meanwhile GLORIA takes the wheelchair, puts it outside the caravan door and opens it up.)*

| | |
|---|---|
| GLORIA | I'd best get the ramp down. *(She takes the wooden ramp from under the table and puts it outside the caravan door. PAULA and DEN reach the door. GLORIA gets outside the door to help DEN slowly down the ramp and they both seat him in the wheelchair. He is exhausted by the effort.)* |
| PAULA | You alright, Dad? |
| DEN | Aye. Just wait while I get me breath. |
| PAULA | Nice deep breaths, if you can, Dad. |
| DEN | I'm trying love. I'm trying. Nice warm night isn't it? |
| GLORIA | Yes love. And look at them stars! You don't get that in town! |
| DEN | Bloody hell! Look at that! Millions of them! By God, it makes you feel small, doesn't it Glo? |
| GLORIA | Yes. My old gran used to say that every one of them stars is someone that you loved that passed on. |
| PAULA | Mum! |
| DEN | No. You're alright, Paula. I like that idea. It makes more sense to me than heaven or hell. You know, becoming part of the universe. Out there, in your own little space. Shining away. Right! I'm ready to be moved. And take it easy, this time, our kid. You nearly tipped me out of this thing yesterday. |
| PAULA | Don't exaggerate. |
| DEN | I'm not exaggerating. You're bloody lethal behind a wheelchair. I don't know how the patients in that hospital of yours survive. You're like a bull in a china shop. |
| PAULA | Shut up and fasten your seat belt. |

*(She turns the wheelchair around and DEN keeps saying "Steady, steady". GLORIA lingers behind.)*

GLORIA     *(calling off)* I'll be there in a minute love. I just want to spend a penny! *(She goes back in the caravan, slumps down on the bed and looks lost. She picks up DEN'S spectacles and folds them.)*

GLORIA     Daft bugger's forgotten his specs. I'd better put them in my handbag, otherwise I'll forget them too. *(She starts crying softly. PAULA comes back, all excited.)*

PAULA     Oh Mum, hurry up! You missed the best bit! Everyone cheered and clapped when I wheeled Dad in! You should have been there! *(She realizes her Mum is crying)* Oh Mum. What is it? Is it getting too much for you? *(She sits next to GLORIA and puts her arm round her. GLORIA cries a bit more, then wipes her tears.)*

GLORIA     Oh, it's daft really. I shouldn't give in to it. Only, just lately, your Dad's been getting down...you know...and he's been saying things. I have a job to keep a smile on my face sometimes.

PAULA     What's he been saying?

GLORIA     Oh, just things about dying. He's worrying about me. I told him not to but...well...we've been together for so long, love. He knows I'm going to be lost without him.

PAULA     Of course he does. But he knows you've got us. Me and Peter and Brian. And now Hannah.

GLORIA     *(smiling)* And now Hannah. I know. But still... Do you know what he said to me tonight? He said he was sorry that I'd only had a two-berth life.

| | |
|---|---|
| PAULA | What does that mean? |
| GLORIA | He meant the caravan. Only being two-berth because we could never afford to get a bigger one. He said he wished that he'd been able to give me a better life. |
| PAULA | That's silly. |
| GLORIA | I know! I couldn't have had a better life with any man, Paula. Your father's been a kind, generous, loving man all through our marriage. That's why it's going to be so hard to lose him. |
| PAULA | I know Mum. I know. |
| GLORIA | What makes it worse is that he's so sharp. His mind's as sharp as a razor. I marvel, all the time, at him. He knows everything, he reads everything. He's the wisest man I know and, sometimes, it just doesn't seem fair. |
| PAULA | You know he doesn't have much longer Mum, don't you? |
| GLORIA | Yes, love. And so does your Dad. We both know he's living on borrowed time. Still, he said we can book up the Scarborough trip next month. |
| PAULA | He may not make it to next month. |
| GLORIA | *(gently)* No. Don't say that. Always plan. Always hope. That's how your Dad and I have lived our lives and that's how we're going to face his death. |
| PAULA | OK. Why don't you stay here and have a bit of a rest? I'll tell Dad you've got a headache or something. |
| GLORIA | No you won't! I've had my little cry and now I'm going to put some lippy on and go in that hall. I want to see my family win that hamper! |

| | |
|---|---|
| PAULA | Dad'll win it for us. |
| GLORIA | Of course he will. Your Dad's a bloody marvel. Come on lass! Up and at 'em! I've got a man to cheer on, a trip to Scarborough to book and...now...I've got a wedding to plan as well! There's always something to do eh? |
| PAULA | You're a miracle, Mum. |
| GLORIA | Don't be daft. It's your Dad who's the miracle. I just latch on to his strength. Always have. But I'm frightened I'll just be a shell when he goes. I won't be a person anymore. |
| PAULA | Now you're being daft. You musn't think like that, because the rest of the family need you. Who's going to babysit all the grandchildren? |
| GLORIA | *(with a sharp but hopeful intake of breath)* You're not...? |
| PAULA | No. Not yet. But I've stopped taking the pill and it's just a matter of time. Peter said that now he's got that promotion, it's a good time to start a family. And, as for our Brian – he's so gormless, I wouldn't be surprised if he starts a family on his honeymoon! |
| | *(GLORIA smiles and hugs PAULA.)* |
| GLORIA | As long as I'm needed, I'll be OK. Now! Best foot forward our Paula! I want that hamper! |
| | *(They leave)* |

*MUSIC*

*FADE LIGHTS*

# FURNITURE LIST

Throughout:          fitted interior of a small caravan, as per the description in
                     the script and the set plan.

# PROPERTY LIST

On set
throughout:          DEN's shoes and socks *(under the dining table or in a
                     cupboard)*; several pillows; travel rug; portable TV;
                     ordinary kettle or electric kettle; two mugs; canister or box
                     of teabags; bottle or carton of milk; sugar; newspaper *(on
                     dining table)*; DEN's reading glasses *(on dining table)*; pen
                     *(on dining table)*; medical drip on stand, attached to DEN's
                     arm; folded- up wheelchair; wooden ramp *(under dining
                     table)*.

Page 1:              GLORIA: enters with handbag containing handkerchief,
                     her reading glasses and a quiz sheet.

Page 2:              GLORIA: hands DEN a sheet of questions.

Page 3:              GLORIA: hands DEN his reading glasses from the dining
                     table.

Page 5:              PAULA: enters with two cheese ploughmans on plates.

Page 9:              GLORIA: gets handkerchief from her handbag.

Page 10:             GLORIA: gets her reading glasses from her handbag.

Page 12:             BRIAN: appears with half a pint of Guinness.

Page 26:             GLORIA: takes her handbag and DEN's reading glasses
                     offstage.

# LIGHTING AND EFFECTS PLOT

Music at beginning and end.

Page 1:            Switch the lights on. Concentrated lighting on the
                   "caravan". The rest of the stage should be in darkness, as it
                   is supposed to be night outside. A little ambient light
                   around the "caravan" for the benefit of any action that
                   takes place "outside" *(like Page 23)*.

Page 26:           Bring up music, fade lights.


No sound effects.

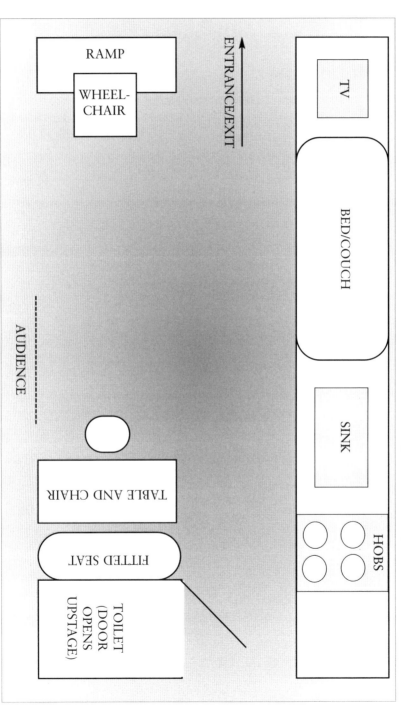

A TWO BERTH LIFE – SET PLAN (aerial view)